The Urbana Free Library

To renew: call **217-367-4057**
or go to **urbanafreelibrary.org**
and select **My Account**

FORENSIC INVESTIGATIONS
OF THE
ANCIENT CHINESE

Heather C. Hudak

CRABTREE
PUBLISHING COMPANY
WWW.CRABTREEBOOKS.COM

Author: Heather C. Hudak

Editors: Sarah Eason, John Andrews,
    Petrice Custance, and Janine Deschenes

Proofreader and indexer: Wendy Scavuzzo

Editorial director: Kathy Middleton

Design: Paul Myerscough, Paul Oakley,
    and Jane McKenna

Cover design: Paul Myerscough

Photo research: Rachel Blount

**Production coordinator and
    Prepress technician:** Tammy McGarr

Print coordinator: Katherine Berti

Consultant: John Malam

Produced for Crabtree Publishing Company by
Calcium Creative Ltd.

Library and Archives Canada Cataloguing in Publication

Hudak, Heather C., 1975-, author
        Forensic investigations of the ancient Chinese /
Heather C. Hudak.

(Forensic footprints of ancient worlds)
Includes index.
Issued in print and electronic formats.
ISBN 978-0-7787-4940-0 (hardcover).--
ISBN 978-0-7787-4953-0 (softcover).--
ISBN 978-1-4271-2113-4 (HTML)

        1. China--Antiquities--Juvenile literature. 2. Forensic
archaeology--China--Juvenile literature. 3. Archaeology and
history--China--Juvenile literature. I. Title.

DS719.H833 2018   j931.00909   C2018-902975-7
                                             C2018-902976-5

Library of Congress Cataloging-in-Publication Data

Names: Hudak, Heather C., 1975- author.
Title: Forensic investigations of the ancient Chinese /
    Heather C. Hudak.
Description: New York, N.Y. : Crabtree Publishing Company,
    2019. | Series: Forensic footprints of ancient worlds |
    Includes index.
Identifiers: LCCN 2018027909 (print) | LCCN 2018031059 (ebook) |
    ISBN 9781427121134 (Electronic) |
    ISBN 9780778749400 (hardcover) |
    ISBN 9780778749530 (pbk.)
Subjects: LCSH: Forensic archaeology--China--Juvenile literature.
    | Forensic anthropology--China--Juvenile literature. |
    Excavations (Archaeology)--China--Juvenile literature. | China-
    -Antiquities--Juvenile literature.
Classification: LCC CC79.F67 (ebook) |
    LCC CC79.F67 H83 2019 (print) | DDC 931--dc23
LC record available at https://lccn.loc.gov/2018027909

Crabtree Publishing Company

www.crabtreebooks.com   1-800-387-7650

Printed in the U.S.A./092018/CG20180719

Published in Canada
Crabtree Publishing
616 Welland Ave.
St. Catharines, Ontario
L2M 5V6

Published in the United States
Crabtree Publishing
PMB 59051
350 Fifth Avenue, 59th Floor
New York, New York 10118

Published in the United Kingdom
Crabtree Publishing
Maritime House
Basin Road North, Hove
BN41 1WR

Published in Australia
Crabtree Publishing
3 Charles Street
Coburg North
VIC, 3058

CONTENTS

INVESTIGATING ANCIENT CHINA

China is a huge country in Asia. Its **civilization** began more than 5,000 years ago, and China quickly became one of the smartest and most powerful civilizations of the ancient world. The early Chinese were hunters who lived in caves. Over time, they began to farm the land and raise animals.

Rise of the Dynasties

Early Chinese people built villages and lived in small family groups called clans. As the villages grew into cities and towns, the clans got bigger. They developed into powerful **dynasties** that lasted from 1600 B.C.E. to 1912 C.E. These dynasties ruled ancient China, but who were they and what do we know about them?

Some of what we know about the ancient Chinese comes from **evidence** they left behind. This includes **artifacts** (objects from the past), buildings, and writings. Their **emperors** (heads of the great dynasties) were buried in huge tombs. The tombs were filled with objects that tell us a lot about ancient Chinese life and beliefs. One tomb contained 8,000 life-size **clay** soldiers, called the **Terracotta** Army. Why were they there? Is there a way to solve this and other mysteries about ancient China? Yes—with **forensic science**!

⌃ *By examining artifacts, such as this bronze head, forensic scientists can find clues about the tools used by craftspeople in ancient China.*

Forensic tests on human bones can identify how old the person was and if they were male or female.

HOW SCIENCE SOLVED THE PAST:

FORENSIC FOOTPRINTS

To solve crimes, forensic scientists examine evidence from the places where crimes took place, called **crime scenes**. The **techniques** that they use to solve crimes are also used to solve mysteries about the past. **Archaeologists** and **anthropologists** study the clues, or forensic footprints, ancient people left behind to find out more about them. Archaeologists use forensic techniques to find out more about ancient buildings and **sites**. Anthropologists use forensic techniques to learn more about ancient peoples from their skeletons and the objects they left behind.

The ancient Chinese tried to predict the future using bones called oracle bones. This ox bone dates from between 1600 and 1000 B.C.E. Priests used red-hot pokers to make the holes in the bone (see below).

DID
You Know?

Scientists have discovered ox bones and turtle shells that ancient Chinese emperors used to speak with their **ancestors**! In front of the bone or shell, the emperor asked his ancestors a question. To get a reply, his priest pressed a red-hot poker into the bone or shell. Depending on how it cracked, the answer was either "yes" or "no."

SOLVING PAST MYSTERIES

Just as forensic scientists can help police locate a body in a crime scene, they can also find out where bodies were buried long ago. They dig up items buried with the bodies, carefully make note of them, and **preserve** them. They use forensic science to find out more about the bodies and items.

Raiding the Remains

Just as forensic scientists study skeletons or bodies to solve mysteries about a crime, they also study ancient **remains** to find out more about people who lived long ago. They carry out tests to find out when and why they died. They can even use computers to create face shapes from ancient skulls.

Scientists were amazed when they found the coffin of Lady Dai, who died in 163 B.C.E. Her body (shown left) was well preserved and even had blood in its veins! Using forensic techniques, scientists created a model of Lady Dai as she might have looked aged 30.

So, what clues, or forensic footprints, did the ancient Chinese leave behind and what can we learn from them? Let's follow their forensic footprint trail!

DID
You Know?

Skulls and bones of young women were found in burial pits near the Terracotta Army (see page 12). Experts are scanning the skulls and bones and building a picture of them on a computer. This will help experts find out who the women were. It also means they have a picture of the remains in case the original bones are damaged.

HOW SCIENCE SOLVED THE PAST:
MODELING MYSTERIES

We cannot visit the past, but we can model it. Forensic scientists use clues from ancient sites to figure out how the buildings that once stood there looked. For example, **foundations** in the ground hint at where walls might have been. Broken pottery could mean a garbage site. Using this information, archaeologists work on a computer to create a **three-dimensional (3-D)** model of the site as it might once have been. This helps them learn about how the buildings were made and what they might have been used for.

Forensic scientists can also use clues from the past to make 3-D models of people who lived long ago. They study skulls and skeletons to figure out what a person looked like. They then use that information to create a 3-D model of the person.

When ancient remains such as bones are uncovered, forensic scientists have to treat them carefully so they do not break or crumble.

THE GREAT WALL OF CHINA

A huge wall, called the "Great Wall," stretches across part of present-day China. The wall was first built in small sections made of earth and stones. Then the sections were joined and made longer and stronger, using materials such as granite, limestone, and brick. Some experts think the wall is up to 12,500 miles (20,117 km) long, but no one knows exactly how long it is or how it was built.

DID You Know?

The Great Wall has been called the longest graveyard in the world. Thousands of workers died building the wall—about one for every 5 feet (1.5 m) of wall built! Some people even believed that the bones of the dead workers had been mixed into the wall's **mortar** (material used to hold bricks together). However, forensic scientists have proved this is wrong. Chemical tests show that the bricks are held together mainly by rice flour!

Scientific tests have shown that the Great Wall was built in sections. By forensically testing the age of the materials used, scientists think the wall took about 2,000 years to build.

Finding Parts of the Wall

Archaeologists are using forensic technology to find hidden sections of the Great Wall. **Lidar** devices fire **laser** light at a target, then measure the time it takes for the light beams to reflect, or bounce back. Forensic investigators use lidar to create amazingly realistic 3-D pictures of crime scenes, which they can study later in detail or use as evidence in court. Scientists attach lidar devices to **drones** or aircraft. In flight, the devices send pulses of light into the land to create 3-D images of any wall hidden underground. If any wood is found in the wall, forensic scientists can then use **carbon dating** to figure out how old it is. Carbon dating measures how much of a substance called carbon there is in an **organic** material, which tells experts how old it is.

HOW SCIENCE SOLVED THE PAST:

SKELETON CREW

Skeletons of the workers who built the Great Wall have been found buried along it—but who were these people? Forensic scientists are studying their bones to find out more. By doing so, they will be able to figure out where the people came from, how they lived, and how old they were when they died. If a skull is in good condition, experts can make a 3-D model of a face. It means we can see just what a Great Wall worker looked like.

Scientists are studying skeletons found along the Great Wall to learn if the workers died from natural causes or from accidents.

TALES FROM THE TOMB

The ancient Chinese believed in a life after death, called the **afterlife.** To help people on their journey into the afterlife, they were buried with things they might need, such as food, clothes, jewelry, and even their servants—who were killed as **sacrifices!** Emperors were buried in large tomb sites that contained many different rooms. One tomb even had a restroom!

Talking Bones

When they examine tombs, archaeologists study the bones of any skeletons they find to try to figure out who the bones might have belonged to. At a crime scene, forensic investigators use tiny parts of any bones and teeth they find to identify a victim. These tiny parts, invisible to the eye, are called **isotopes.** Forensic scientists can test the isotopes in ancient bones and teeth to figure out what sort of diet people had, and even where they were born. To test isotopes, scientists cut small pieces of bone into thin sections. They then **analyze** the isotopes in the sections under a **microscope.** They also analyze them using a special piece of equipment called a **spectrometer.**

DID You Know?

The early Chinese were **nomads.** This means they had no fixed home and traveled around all the time. As time passed, they settled in one place and became farmers. By studying the bones of these people and their animals, scientists can figure out when the ancient Chinese became farmers. The scientists study a material inside bones called **DNA.** DNA is found in all living things. It can tell scientists how far people traveled, if they went over land or by sea, and where they settled. This helps build a picture of how the ancient Chinese civilization grew.

Forensic tools can be used to see the body inside this 2,000-year-old jade burial suit. Because the suit does not need to be removed, neither it nor the body are damaged.

HOW SCIENCE SOLVED THE PAST:

SECRETS OF THE TOMB

The Shang Dynasty ruled China from around 1600 to 1046 B.C.E. Their tombs contain many bones. But who did the bones belong to? Rulers and other important people were buried with their sacrificed servants so they could be looked after on their journey to the afterlife. Forensic scientists can examine the bones to find out the age of these people, how they died, and even what kind of diet they had.

This statue, made to protect a tomb from thieves, can be forensically tested to find out where and how it was made.

Scientists take sample pieces from skulls found in royal tombs and use the latest technology, such as spectrometers, to find clues as to how the people died.

THE TERRACOTTA ARMY

In 1974, farmers digging a water well discovered one of the most amazing archaeological sites ever. It was the tomb of Qin Shi Huang, the first Chinese emperor, who died in 210 B.C.E. He was buried with more than 8,000 soldiers, 130 chariots, and 520 horses, all made of terracotta clay. They became known as the Terracotta Army.

Armed with Arrows

The warriors were armed with more than 40,000 arrowheads and hundreds of **crossbow triggers**. They also had swords, spears, and other types of weapons. Scientists tested all the weapons in the tomb, including the arrowheads. They used a handheld **X-ray** scanner to test chemicals on the arrowheads. Forensic investigators also use this type of scanner to test objects found at crime scenes, such as a bag that might contain a bomb.

Using the scanner, the scientists at the tomb could test the weapons quickly and without damaging them. Their tests showed that although the arrows were all similar in shape and size, they contained slightly different metals. This showed that the arrowheads had been made in batches at different workshops.

When this handheld scanner is pointed at an object, it detects what chemicals the object contains. Forensic scientists can use scanners to find blood, metals, and other substances on artifacts.

*The ancient Chinese used **chromium**, a silvery substance, to cover the swords discovered with the Terracotta Army (see opposite).*

DID
You Know?

The ancient Chinese **mass-produced**, or made a large number of, items just like a factory does today! Scientists found that each crossbow trigger from the tomb was made of three parts. When they compared crossbows, they found that their parts were identical. This proved that the ancient Chinese had smart ways of making hundreds of the same sort of item to exactly the same style and standard.

HOW SCIENCE SOLVED THE PAST:
SUPER SWORDS

The swords in the tomb were in very good condition. How had they survived so well for so long? Forensic tests revealed that the surface of the swords contained a layer of chromium, a material that protected the weapons from rusting. In the 1920s, a similar technology was introduced in the United States. Amazingly, the ancient Chinese had developed it more than 2,000 years earlier!

« *Forensic scientists used a wide range of tests on the terracotta soldiers (below) as well as on their weapons. The soldiers were equipped with crossbow triggers (left) and swords (right).* »

A COLORFUL COLLECTION

Today, the Terracotta Army looks gray, brown, and beige. However, when the warriors were created, they were painted in different colors. The archaeologists who first uncovered the warriors soon realized that their work was destroying the colorful paint. Buried for thousands of years, the paint layers had become "stuck" to the earth that surrounded them. When archaeologists started to dig up the figures, the layers of paint flaked away, leaving just the clay models. Archaeologists turned to forensic scientists to find a way to stop this from happening.

Flaking Off

Forensic scientists use techniques called **gas chromatography** and **mass spectrometry** to find substances such as drugs and explosives at a crime scene. In gas chromatography, tiny samples are taken from objects and turned into a gas. The gas is then analyzed to see what the sample is made of. In mass spectrometry, machines separate tiny samples into even smaller parts, then analyze them. The same forensic tests have shown that the Terracotta Army models were first covered in a layer of **lacquer** to protect them. Then the models were painted in different colors. Many different colors were used, such as purple, red, green, blue, white, and black. Testing even shows what colors were used where. For example, pink was used for the face and hands. With this knowledge, archaeologists can now separate the colored lacquer from the earth and reattach it to the models.

This statue of a monk from around 500 C.E. has been painted in colors that can still be seen. Forensic tests will reveal the hidden colors.

The **mineral** cinnabar was ground into a powder to make red paint in ancient China. By testing artifacts for the presence of minerals, scientists can identify what colors the artifacts may once have been painted.

Using the paint fragments found on a terracotta warrior today (left), scientists can create a model (top right) of how the soldier would have originally looked.

HOW SCIENCE SOLVED THE PAST:

MAKING THE PAINT

All paints need something to **bind** their chemicals together. But how did the ancient Chinese bind their paints? Forensic scientists used gas chromatography and mass spectrometry to test different samples of the paint they found on the warriors. The results showed that the ancient Chinese used egg to bind their paints!

DID You Know?

Archaeologists use plastic wrap—but not for food! Because of the type of paints used on the terracotta figures, they quickly become covered in **mold** when they are exposed to the air. Thanks to forensic science, archaeologists have developed ways to preserve the figures. They are now sprayed with an **antifungal** liquid and quickly wrapped in plastic wrap.

RETURN FROM THE DEAD

The tomb of Emperor Qin Shi Huang also contained the skeletons of many women. Historians wondered what they looked like when they were alive. They knew what the terracotta warriors looked like because they were all modeled in clay. But how could they tell what the women looked like from their skeletons alone? Luckily, forensic science had the answers!

Making Faces

Forensic scientists use 3-D **digital** scanning to create models from skulls and bones. Scientists used this technique to model the skulls of the women found at the Terracotta Army site. The lifelike models clearly showed how the women once looked. By modeling them, the scientists also preserved the skeletons. Bones and skulls found buried in tombs can **decay** when exposed to air and daylight. Models never decay. By modeling skeletons, they are preserved forever.

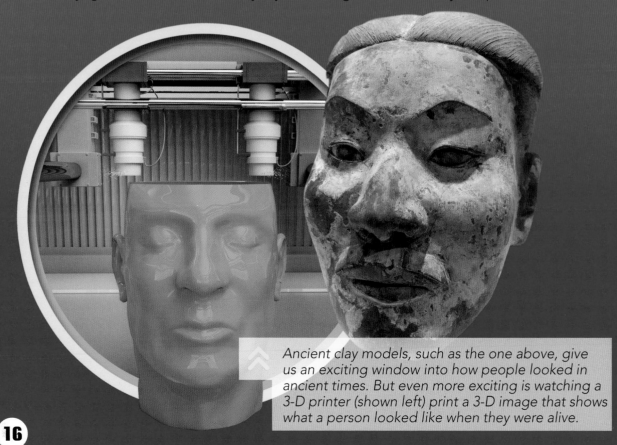

Ancient clay models, such as the one above, give us an exciting window into how people looked in ancient times. But even more exciting is watching a 3-D printer (shown left) print a 3-D image that shows what a person looked like when they were alive.

Scientists scanned the ears of the terracotta soldiers and discovered that no two pairs were the same. This could mean that the soldiers were modeled on real people!

LOOKING SOLDIERS IN THE FACE

Each of the terracotta warriors has a different expression on his face. Were they modeled on real men or did the **sculptors** choose whatever facial features they liked? Forensic scientists can use ears to identify people in a similar way that fingerprints are used to identify criminals. Researchers photographed the ears of 30 terracotta warriors and used the images to create 3-D models on a computer. The models can even tell historians if some of the features on the faces of the warriors were copied from the faces of people who lived in different countries.

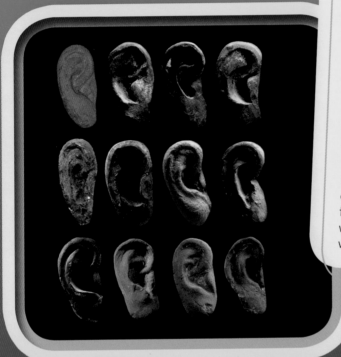

To **reconstruct** a face from an ancient skull, a scientist scans the skull with a hand-held scanner. He or she then sends the scan images to a computer. The computer creates a 3-D image of the head. The image is sent to a 3-D printer. The printer then prints a 3-D model of the skull. Next, clay is used to model the muscles and details of the face. The shapes of the eyes and nose are based on information experts already have about what ancient peoples looked like.

Acrobat models were also found in the emperor's tomb. Scientists are studying them to find out if they were from China or elsewhere (see below).

DID You Know?

The acrobat figures in the emperor's tomb were put there to entertain him during his journey to the afterlife. Some experts think the models do not look like Chinese people. They believe they look like people from Myanmar, a country next to China that used to be called Burma.

RICE, TEA, AND ANCIENT DUMPLINGS

The soil on an archaeological site has been there since ancient times. This soil often contains the remains of food, such as bones and seeds. Forensic scientists can test these soil samples to figure out what food people ate in ancient China.

Floating to the Top

Forensic investigators use a technique called **flotation** to study soil from a crime scene. Scientists use the same technique to discover secrets about the ancient Chinese. In flotation, dried soil is placed on a **mesh** screen. Water is gently bubbled up through the soil. When this happens, light materials such as seeds, **pollen**, and **charcoal** float up to the surface of the water. Tiny pieces of heavier material, such as bone, are left behind on the screen. Scientists can then analyze these heavier materials.

Forensic scientists take samples from different layers of soil to test for food, pollen, and other remains.

In one archaeological site, scientists studied soil from ancient garbage pits where animal bones and household waste had been thrown. They carried out flotation tests on the soil and found seeds, such as rice seeds. Nutshells, soybeans, root vegetables, and burned wood were also found. This evidence not only showed what the ancient Chinese ate, but also that they cooked it.

By studying rice seeds, scientists can tell if they are from farmed rice or wild rice. This tells scientists when ancient people began to grow rice, and therefore when modern-day farming began in ancient China.

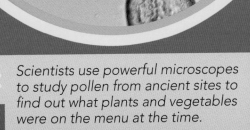

Scientists use powerful microscopes to study pollen from ancient sites to find out what plants and vegetables were on the menu at the time.

Artifacts found on ancient sites, such as this 8,000-year-old jar, are scanned. They are then tested with chemicals that can help scientists identify the remains of any food or drink inside the artifacts. »

DID
You Know?

Archaeologists have discovered ancient dumplings that are 1,700 years old! Dried into rock-like objects, the dumplings were found in tombs, where dry conditions kept them from decaying. Forensic scientists will analyze the world's oldest dumplings to find out more about them!

WORLDS UNDERWATER

Along with ancient sites, archaeologists also explore **shipwrecks**. These are sunken ships found at the bottom of the ocean. In 2007, a Chinese **cargo** ship around 1,000 years old was discovered in the South China Sea. More than 14,000 objects have been found in the wreck, such as gold and silver artifacts, copper coins, and **porcelain** pots. Forensic science can help historians find shipwrecks and learn about their cargo.

Searching for Shipwrecks

A crime scene can be underwater. Forensic investigators use the **Global Positioning System (GPS)** and **sonar** techniques to find ships, airplanes, and other vehicles in oceans, rivers, or lakes. Archaeologists also use GPS and sonar to find underwater sites. Using **satellites** in space, GPS shows roughly where a wreck might be. Sonar readings on a boat can then find the wreck's exact location.

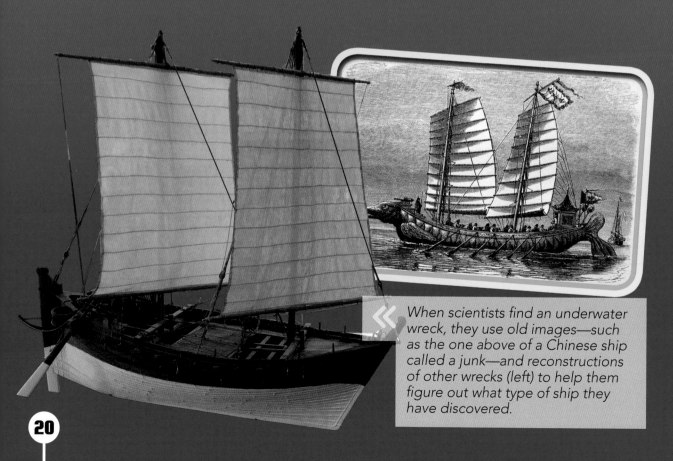

When scientists find an underwater wreck, they use old images—such as the one above of a Chinese ship called a junk—and reconstructions of other wrecks (left) to help them figure out what type of ship they have discovered.

Once the wreck is found, scientists can use **remotely operated** vehicles (ROVs) fitted with powerful cameras to take a look around the ship. The scientists then make a 3-D model of the wreck on their computers. Sometimes, pieces of artifacts are buried in the ground underneath or near a wreck. To find these artifacts, forensic experts use a piece of equipment called a **sub-bottom profiler**, which uses pulses of sound to find hidden objects that can then be dug up.

DID
You Know?

The wood a boat is made from can tell forensic experts where the boat was built. Tests can tell if the wood is from a tree that grew in a **temperate** (mild) or **tropical** (hot) **climate**. By examining **cross sections** of the wood and the **resin** found in the wood, scientists can tell which tree the wood is from and where the tree grows. This helps historians trace the country that built the boat.

ROV-3350
REMOTELY OPERATED VEHICLE

HOW SCIENCE SOLVED THE PAST:
A SHIP'S SECRETS

Using underwater scanning and measuring techniques, scientists can learn a lot about how a ship was built, where it came from, and what type of ship it was—for example, a warship or a cargo ship. Rings, bracelets, and other jewelry were found on the Chinese cargo shipwreck discovered in 2007. This means that there were people onboard other than sailors. They may have been **merchants** traveling with their wives.

Underwater exploration can be dangerous in rough seas or deep down on the ocean floor. Scientists use robots, such as the remotely operated vehicle shown above, to explore shipwrecks and send back images. The images can then be made into 3-D images of the wreck. The robots can also pick up samples and artifacts for testing.

JADE WORKSHOP

Jade is a stone that has been used for many thousands of years to make objects such as jewelry and statues. In ancient China, jade was thought to have magical powers. It was believed that it protected people on their journeys to the afterlife. To the Chinese, jade was even more precious than gold! Lumps of jade stone were carved by hand into beautiful objects. Discovering the techniques and tools that the ancient Chinese used to make jade objects can tell us much about their civilization.

HOW SCIENCE SOLVED THE PAST:

CARVED WONDERS

Scientists analyze jade objects using electron microscopes. They look for marks on the objects that show what type of tools were used to make them. In ancient China, jade objects were carved using light tools that drilled holes in jade and shaped it. The people who used these tools were very skilled. No marks were found to show that heavier tools such as saws or chisels were used.

In ancient China, lumps of jade such as the one below were carved into beautiful objects by highly skilled craftspeople.

Forensic scientists examine pieces of jade objects to find out how they were made. Discovering how a civilization created objects and the tools they used can help experts build a picture of life at that time.

Jade Trail

Forensic scientists use a combination of methods to study jade objects found in tombs and other ancient sites in China. From this, they can figure out how and when the objects were made and where the jade came from. Scientists use **infrared** light and X-rays to look deep inside an object without damaging it. They also study the surface of the jade object, using powerful microscopes to spot tool marks on the surface that are invisible to the eye.

Scientists also examine objects using a **scanning electron microscope (SEM)**. This type of microscope uses laser beams of light to "scan" the surface of an object and pick up things other microscopes cannot see, such as the tiniest marks made by a tool. Forensic investigators also use SEMs to find clues on the surface of objects taken from a crime scene, such as markings on bullets or fingerprints on bank notes.

This 1,000-year-old cup made from jade has animals carved into it, such as the tiger peering over the edge. Objects such as this one were very precious in ancient China and were a symbol of wealth and power. Forensic scientists can use X-rays and infrared light to study jade artifacts to see how, where, and when they were made.

DID
You Know?

Some Chinese emperors and other important people were buried in suits made from thousands of pieces of jade (see page 10). The pieces were joined together with gold, silver, or silk thread. The ancient Chinese believed such a suit would offer protection in the afterlife. Jade pieces were even put in the person's ears, nose, and mouth!

THE BLOOD POOL

Archaeologists have discovered a site called Yongshan Blood Pool. It is filled with the skeletons of more than 600 horses, many lying side by side. Why had so many horses been killed? In 2016, archaeologists dug deeper and found many pits filled with animal bones. They also found more than 2,000 artifacts, including chariots. In ancient China, horses were highly prized. The archaeologists figured out that the site was used by Chinese emperors more than 2,000 years ago to make animal sacrifices to their gods.

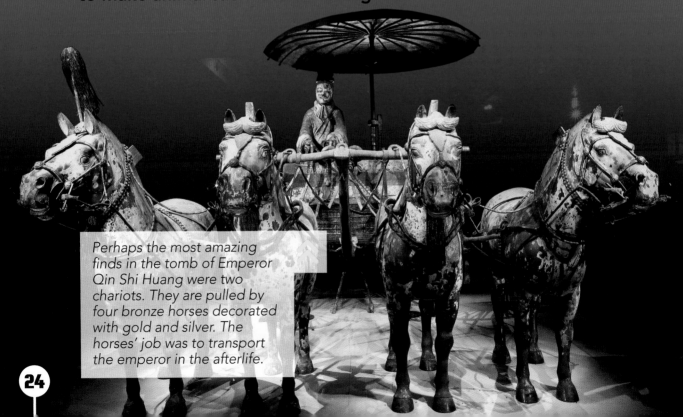

Perhaps the most amazing finds in the tomb of Emperor Qin Shi Huang were two chariots. They are pulled by four bronze horses decorated with gold and silver. The horses' job was to transport the emperor in the afterlife.

Skull and Bones

Horse, cattle, pig, and dog bones are often found in ancient Chinese tombs. To identify an animal, forensic scientists first look at the skull. Horse and cow skulls are similar in shape, but horse skulls are much smaller than cow skulls. A cow skull is also flatter and wider at the front. Sheep and pig skulls are roughly the same size, but pig skulls are longer and flatter. Some animals, including horses, have eye sockets at the sides of their heads. Animals such as dogs have eye sockets at the fronts of their heads. Further forensic tests such as carbon dating can be carried out to find the age of the bones.

Horses were considered lucky in ancient China, so wealthy and powerful people were buried with statues of horses.

Forensic scientists piece together animal skulls found in tombs. A horse skull (above) is long and slender, with broad, flat teeth that can be seen even more clearly on an X-ray (below).

HOW SCIENCE SOLVED THE PAST:

TALKING TEETH

Tooth **enamel**, the outer layer of teeth, is the hardest substance in the body. This is why teeth often survive fires, while other body parts are destroyed or are damaged. Studying teeth can help scientists figure out what animals were buried in ancient Chinese tombs, even if the other remains are damaged. Meat-eating animals have pointed cheek teeth, while plant-eating animals have broad, flat cheek teeth.

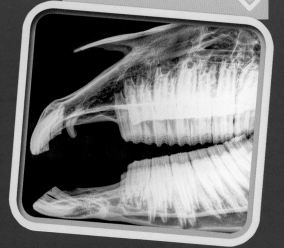

FINDING A NEW HUMAN SPECIES

Human remains, including skulls and teeth, found in caves in southwest China have puzzled historians. Scientists carried out carbon-dating tests on charcoal found in the skulls and discovered that the people they belonged to lived between 11,500 and 14,550 years ago. Scientists also tested teeth, and skull and jaw pieces, and found that the faces of these people were different from those of anyone else in ancient China.

DID You Know?

Scientists studying the teeth from the people in the cave were in for a surprise! They fed their study results into a computer **database** that contains details of the teeth of all known human **species**. The scientists hoped to discover what species the cave people belonged to. But the teeth did not match any of the 5,000 types of teeth on the database. The scientists had found a new kind of human!

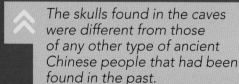

The skulls found in the caves were different from those of any other type of ancient Chinese people that had been found in the past.

HOW SCIENCE SOLVED THE PAST:

HISTORY MYSTERY

When they discovered that they had found a new species of human, scientists were desperate to know who these mysterious people were. They carried out DNA testing on a thighbone found in another cave nearby. It revealed that the bone belonged to a species of human that had lived separately from any other species, thousands of years ago. Historians have only just begun to find out about this new human species, and there are still many more mysteries about them for forensic science to solve!

Looking at Leftovers

Forensic investigators analyze the chemicals in food fragments found at a crime scene to find evidence about a victim or a criminal. Chemical analysis of the burned remains on the inside of cooking pots, or in soil from the ground where food was cooked, can tell scientists what type of food was cooked in ancient times. They can tell, for example, if it was meat, fish, or vegetables, and how it was cooked. This helps historians figure out when people began to fish, hunt, farm, grow, and cook their own food. Forensic evidence shows that large red deer were cooked in the Chinese cave where the human remains were found, so scientists have named the mystery people the Red Deer People.

The ancient Chinese go back even further than the Red Deer People. This is a model of Peking Man, a species of human who lived more than 230,000 years ago. He was one of the first humans to walk upright on two legs.

FORENSIC FUTURE

We may never know all of the details of how the ancient Chinese lived. There are many tombs that have not yet been explored. Who knows what is hidden inside them? However, forensic science techniques are helping us learn more about ancient China than was ever dreamed possible.

Advances in technology are providing us with a fascinating gateway to the past. Scientists are discovering clues they did not even know existed. What might forensic science uncover in the future? Our picture of life in ancient China is becoming clearer with each tiny piece of the puzzle as it is discovered and fitted into place!

DID You Know?

Once ancient Chinese tombs are opened and the objects inside are exposed to air and sunlight, those objects quickly start to decay. However, forensic scientists are finding new ways to keep this from happening. They are using chemicals and new materials to protect artifacts so that tombs and other ancient sites can be opened and their secrets revealed.

This bronze lamp was found in a 2,000-year-old Chinese tomb. There are many thousands more artifacts still hidden in the tomb. Forensic science will help us find them.

CAN FORENSICS SOLVE...?

Here are two of the great still-unsolved mysteries about ancient China and its mighty emperors. Forensic scientists are using forensic footprints to try to solve these mysteries, too!

Murdered Princes

The tomb that contains the Terracotta Army was made for Emperor Qin Shi Huang—but his body has never been found. He may be buried in a sealed room at the center of a huge system of 90 rooms. Archaeologists and historians have learned from written records that one of the emperor's sons killed his brothers so he could rule after his father's death. Skeletons have been found in the tomb with their skulls split open by the force of an arrow. DNA and isotope bone testing may reveal if these are the murdered princes and show exactly how they died.

Secrets of the Tomb

In 2015, archaeologists discovered a cemetery that is more than 2,000 years old. It contains eight tombs, temples, and a chariot burial site. Could this be the tomb of Emperor Liu He, who was forced off the throne after only 27 days because he was such a bad ruler? So far, experts have uncovered musical instruments and artifacts made from gold, silver, and jade. They have also found precious jewels, sacrificed horses, sealed coffins, and ancient writings. Archaeologists will call in forensic experts to study all of these amazing artifacts to help reveal the mysteries of the tombs and who they were built for.

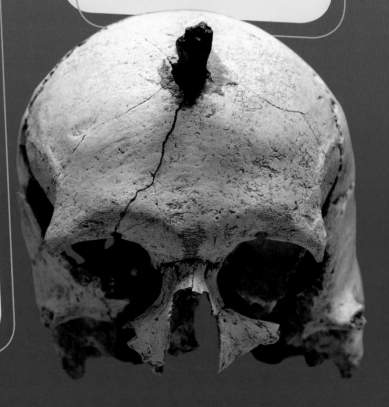

GLOSSARY

Please note: Some **bold-faced** words are defined where they appear in the book.

acrobat A person who entertains others by doing tricks such as backflips

analyze Study something carefully

ancestors Relatives who died long ago

anthropologists Experts who study who ancient people were, how they lived, and where they came from

antifungal A substance used to keep something from going moldy

archaeologists Experts who study where ancient people lived and the things they left behind

bind Join together

cargo The goods that a ship carries

charcoal A hard, black material made by burning wood

chromium A metal-like substance that can be added to metals to make them shinier and more hard-wearing

civilization A settled and stable community in which people live together peacefully and use systems such as writing to communicate

clay A heavy, sticky material that can be shaped easily and becomes hard when baked

climate The type of weather a place has over a long period of time

cross sections What you see of objects when they have been cut open

crossbow triggers The levers pulled to fire a crossbow—a weapon that fires short arrows

database A record of information kept on a computer that can be shared

decay Rot

digital Information, such as a picture, that can be seen on a computer

DNA Material that contains all of the information needed to create an individual living thing

drones Unmanned aircraft guided by remote control or onboard computers

dynasties Lines of rulers who come from the same family

evidence Facts and information that tell us if something is true

forensic science The use of scientific methods and techniques to find clues about crimes or the past

foundations Solid structures that support a building from underneath

Global Positioning System (GPS) A system using satellites in space that can help find the position of places on Earth

infrared A type of light that feels warm but cannot be seen

isotopes Different forms of a chemical

lacquer A clear liquid painted on wood and other surfaces to protect them from damage

laser A narrow, concentrated beam of light

merchants People who buy and sell products in large amounts, especially by trading

mesh A material made from wire with small holes that allow water to pass through

microscope A device that is used to see objects that are too small to be seen by the naked eye

mineral A substance that is naturally formed under the ground

mold A fuzzy substance that grows on things that are damp and decaying

mortar The material used to hold bricks in place when building a wall

organic Something that is, or was, living

pollen A fine powder that is part of a plant

porcelain A hard, white material made by baking fine clay

preserve Make sure something stays the same

reconstruct To put something together again to make it as it was

remains Bodies, bones, objects, or parts of objects left over from the past

remotely operated Operated from a distance using an electric device

resin Thick, sticky liquid that comes from a tree and is often used in medicine

sacrifices Killings carried out to honor an emperor or a god

satellites Machines in space that collect information or are used for communication

sculptors People who make figures out of stone and other materials

sites Places where something is or was

sonar A technique used to find objects, usually underwater

species A group of things or people that belong together

spectrometer A machine that analyzes tiny parts of a substance

techniques Methods of doing particular tasks

terracotta A reddish clay used for making statues and other objects

three-dimensional (3-D) Having or appearing to have length, width, and depth

X-ray A wave of energy that is usually used to create pictures of the inside of the body

LEARNING MORE

Books

Collins, Terry. *Ancient China: An Interactive History Adventure*. Capstone Press, 2013.

Ransom, Candice. *Tools and Treasures of Ancient China*. Lerner Publications, 2014.

Slepian, Curtis. *Ancient China: 305 BC (You Are There!)*. Teacher Created Materials, 2016.

Spilsbury, Louise. *Ancient China* (Analyze the Ancients). Gareth Stevens, 2018.

Websites

www.childrensmuseum.org/blog/10-amazing-facts-about-the-terra-cotta-warriors
The website of the Children's Museum in Indianapolis has amazing facts and figures about the incredible Terracotta Army.

www.dkfindout.com/us/history/ancient-china/terra-cotta-army
Find out loads more about ancient China, the Great Wall, and the Terracotta Army—plus, test your knowledge of ancient China.

www.ducksters.com/history/china/ancient_china.php
The Ducksters education site is filled with information on the life, people, and dynasties of ancient China.

https://video.nationalgeographic.com/video/exploreorg/china-great-wall-eorg
Take a walk along the Great Wall of China and discover its secrets for yourself with this video.

INDEX

About the Author

Heather C. Hudak has written hundreds of children's books about all kinds of topics. She loves traveling the world, learning about new cultures, and sharing her experiences on her blog www.wanderlustwayfarer.com.